# Drunk Driving / DUI

## *A Survival Guide For Motorists*

Attorney
## Dennis A. Bjorklund

# PRAETORIAN PUBLISHING

This publication is intended to provide accurate and authoritative information about the subject matter covered. It is sold with the understanding that the publisher does not render legal, accounting or other professional services. If legal advice or other expert assistance is required, seek the legal services of a competent professional.

Persons using this publication when dealing with specific legal matters should exercise discretion and their own independent judgment, and research original sources of authority and local court rules and procedures.

The publisher and author make no representations concerning the contents of this publication and disclaim any warranties of merchantability or fitness for a particular purpose, or any other liability for reliance upon the contents container herein.

This publication is merely the commencement of dialogue with the readers, and we welcome suggestions to update the book for reprint and future editions. Send all comments to the address hereinbelow.

**Library of Congress Cataloging-in-Publication Data**
Bjorklund, Dennis A.
      Drunk Driving / DUI: A Survival Guide for Motorists

            Bibliography: p.
            Includes index.
            1.      Drunk Driving--United States.      2.      Defense (Criminal procedure)--United States.      I.      Title.

First published in the United States of America in 1999
ISBN:978-0-9679852-0-6

PRAETORIAN PUBLISHING
P.O. Box 5556, Coralville, Iowa  52241-0556

Printed in the United States by Morris Publishing
3212 East Highway 30
Kearney, NE  68847
1-800-650-7888

# AUTHOR BIOGRAPHY

Dennis A. Bjorklund is an attorney specializing in drunk driving defense. He has written the only authoritative drunk driving books aimed at helping motorists protect their legal and constitutional rights against the unlawful infringement of law enforcement officers.

*Drunk Driving Defense: How to Beat the Rap* is a comprehensive synopsis at every phase of a drunk driving case, from the initial police stop through trial, with powerful insight into secret tactics used by law enforcement officers and prosecutors, and effective ways to avoid a conviction.

*Drunk Driving / DUI: A Survival Guide for Motorists* is a summary of the constitutional and statutory rights of motorists involved in a drunk driving case, including a thorough review of the drunk driving laws, criminal penalties, driver's license sanctions, and practical suggestions to avoid future legal problems.

*Drunk Driving Laws: Rules of the Road When Crossing State Lines, 2nd Ed.* is a state-by-state overview of drunk driving laws, encompassing the legal standard for a DUI charge, criminal penalties, driver's license sanctions, implied consent procedures, and chemical testing requirements.

*Preventing A Drunk Driving / DUI Arrest* provides expert advice to private citizens so they can prevent a DUI arrest and is the only book on the market that reveals all the secret tactics used by police officers to profile drunk drivers, implement selective enforcement of the laws, track drivers who leave the scene, evaluate evidence to determine whether a motorist is intoxicated, and much more.

Additional drunk driving-related books that were written specifically for motorists are scheduled for future release. *Drunk Driving and the Driver's License Suspension: How to Get Back on the Road* is intended to simplify the department of transportation bureaucracy so motorists can understand the administrative requirements and procedural aspects necessary to obtain a temporary restricted license (work permit), to calculate suspension periods, and achieve license reinstatement.

The Author has an extensive résumé of scholarly accomplishments, which include writing for the Iowa Law Review and being hand-selected as a distinguished literary contributor to author articles within his area of specialty.

# CONTENTS

# CHARTS

# FOREWORD

Considering the volatile social and political climate, most motorists are likely to experience a drunk driving incident at some point in their lives. In an effort to "solve the problem," police officers, prosecutors, and special interest groups continue to push for legislation comparable to prohibition. As a motorist, the best protection is knowledge--becoming informed about all aspects of a drunk driving charge, from the laws, police procedure, and scientific evidence to witness testimony and trial strategy. This book offers crucial information to assist motorists in understanding and asserting their legal rights.

From the perspective of a lawyer specializing in drunk driving defense, the courts are filled with abundant examples of drivers wrongfully accused of drunk driving. When analyzing how this could occur, many incidents are a direct result of ambiguous drunk driving laws or improperly trained police officers. For instance, the presumption of intoxication at a statutorily prescribed blood-alcohol concentration is not necessarily applicable to every driver. In fact, motorists with higher tolerance levels can drive without exhibiting signs of impairment. Unfortunately, in the eyes of the law, the burden of proof shifts to the motorist. Translated into English, this means the motorist must prove sobriety, which becomes a difficult and expensive endeavor. Moreover, modern-day juries are quick to convict due to massive media attention that distorts the true facts about alcohol-related traffic incidents. Generally, it is the lure of so-called scientific evidence that persuades jurors, not hyperbole from expert witnesses.

Shifting the burden of proof to the defendant has one deplorable consequence--innocent drivers are often forced to plead guilty to a drunk driving charge because they did not know their legal rights at the time of a drunk driving arrest. By reading this book, every motorist has the ability to prevent a wrongful drunk driving charge. This text offers an overview of the drunk driving laws so motorists can understand their legal obligations, protect their constitutional rights, and avoid the consequences of a drunk driving conviction. Every effort was made to analyze typical legal scenarios in an organized, straightforward, and illustrative manner.

The various strategies and suggestions, if seriously contemplated and accurately applied, will enhance the chances of walking away from a drunk driving charge without a criminal conviction. Naturally, the entire book must be read from cover to cover and thoroughly understood. Individual chapters offer insight and useful recommendations that can thwart law enforcement efforts to arrest drunk drivers and impede prosecuting attorneys from getting a conviction. The ultimate purpose is to provide motorists with sufficient information to make an informed decision about drinking and driving.

Since virtually all drunk driving charges are won or lost on the facts, each circumstance offers a unique legal challenge in winning a drunk driving case. In other words, despite offering numerous legal tactics to general hypothetical situations it is impossible to offer definitive answers to every circumstance. The goal is to inform motorists about drunk driving laws and offer effective techniques to obtain a positive result. After reading the book, each motorist should have adequate knowledge to make an informed decision when selecting a qualified, competent lawyer.

When interviewing potential defense attorneys, always remain open and honest, and present all relevant facts. Even seemingly minor details can significantly impact legal defense tactics or the jury verdict. Withholding relevant facts or valuable evidence can prevent defense attorneys from accurately analyzing the case, and ultimately increases the chance of conviction.

Although it seems hard to believe, nothing can prevent a drunk driving *arrest*. Sober drivers have been arrested and convicted of the crime based solely upon an officer testifying about a few subjective sensory observations, such as bloodshot/watery eyes, flushed face, rambling speech, or results from the standard field sobriety tests. In most drunk driving cases there are no witnesses, so the trial is merely the driver's word against the officer's. Since most jurors are inclined to believe the officer, a wrongful conviction is not improbable.

Naturally, asserting your legal rights has consequences--it often requires a trial, legal defense costs, an extensive time commitment, and enduring a harrowing experience. However, the expense is nothing compared to the cost of a criminal conviction--statutory fines, incarceration, probation, increased insurance rates, driver's license suspension, limited employment opportunities, ignition interlock devices, vehicle impoundment or immobilization, and the risk of more severe punishment for a second or subsequent drunk driving offense.

Although every effort was made to provide accurate and up-to-date information, each state legislature is continuously modifying drunk driving laws and the courts are redefining the scope of police authority and drivers' rights. The strategies and suggestions represent legal interpretations of the current law or projections about future judiciary inclinations. To obtain the most current and accurate information, always consult an attorney specializing in drunk driving defense.

# Chapter One

# Drunk Driving

---

# Legally Defined

Although it may seem hard to believe, a person does not have to drink or drive to be arrested for drunk driving. In recent years the legal system has made it easier to obtain a conviction, which has thwarted criminal defense attorneys from adequately representing their clients. Ironically, many motorists are wrongfully convicted of drunk driving, even though the prosecutor lacks evidence of drinking or driving. By understanding the drunk driving laws, motorists can protect their rights and prevent a wrongful conviction.

## Driving - Defined

According to most state laws, a drunk driving conviction is appropriate when the motorist has sufficient control over the vehicle. There is no requirement that the motorist have actual physical control of a motor vehicle. In other words, a person does not have to "drive" to be arrested or convicted of drunk driving. The illustrations are numerous. For instance, a passenger was convicted of drunk driving for sitting behind the wheel of a car buried in mud to the axles. According to the court, despite the car being immovable, there was sufficient control of a vehicle to constitute driving.

**Engine Running.** Many courts believe that a running engine is sufficient control over a vehicle to constitute driving. Much like the prior example, a passenger was convicted of drunk driving even though the vehicle was lodged in 18" of snow at the base of a steep embankment. The driver walked for assistance while the passenger, who remained in the vehicle, occasionally started the engine to stay warm. When an officer arrived, the passenger was in the driver's seat with the motor running, and was charged with drunk driving.

In most instances, it is not considered driving if the keys are in the ignition and the engine is off. However, a drunk driving charge could be filed if the person is passed out in the driver's seat and the vehicle is on the side of the road. Moreover, a drunk driving charge could be filed if the engine is running and the person is sitting in the passenger seat. In both instances, the passenger could technically satisfy the legal definition of driving.

**Informant Reports.** The advent of cellular telephones has increased the frequency of motorists notifying police of potential drunk drivers. Informants have become a vital source of information in the detection of impaired drivers. Nevertheless, police officers must personally observe the erratic driving behavior before instituting a vehicle stop. Unfortunately, a dishonest officer can easily fabricate a traffic violation to justify the vehicle stop.

**Proving Who Was Driving.** In some incidents, to obtain a drunk driving conviction the prosecutor must offer evidence that places the defendant behind the wheel of the vehicle. For example, if the driver leaves the scene of an automobile accident, it may be difficult to prove who was driving. Although any admission about driving can be used against the defendant, the police are still required to gather additional corroborating evidence to prove the defendant was driving.

# Drunk - Defined

The other criminal element is proving the driver was legally drunk at the time the vehicle was being operated. Most states presume motorists are legally intoxicated if their blood-alcohol concentration (BAC) is .10 or more, and in 16 states the legal limit is .08. In addition, statutes often incorporate drugs and medication into the definition of intoxication, so a drunk driving conviction can derive from the use of legal or illegal substances.

By comparing body weight to alcohol consumption, motorists can reasonably predict their BAC. However, many factors affect BAC levels--biological composition, individual metabolism, and alcohol absorption rates. Thus, the charts and illustrative examples only offer a general guideline for responsible drinking. It is always best to know the alcohol content of various drinks and consume less than the amount indicated for your particular weight.

# Monitoring BAC Levels

Alcohol in the stomach absorbs at a slower pace than alcohol in the small intestine. The length of time alcohol remains in the stomach depends upon the beverage consumed, presence of food, biological factors, and stress. When alcohol lingers in the stomach, intoxication is less likely to occur because enzymes and bacteria continuously metabolize alcohol before absorption into the bloodstream.

**Calculating Alcohol Content.** To calculate the percentage of alcohol, divide the alcohol proof by 2. BAC levels are often underestimated when the person is consuming beverages with a higher alcohol content. Chart 1 illustrates the alcohol content of various beverages, while Charts 2 and 3 estimate BAC levels using standard alcoholic beverages: 12-ounce domestic beer, 4-ounce glass of wine, or 1¼-ounce shot of 80 proof alcohol.

BAC levels are often miscalculated due to the amount of alcohol in a drink. Mixed drinks frequently contain more than one shot of booze, or the serving container is misleading (e.g., pint-sized mug of beer, oversized wine glass, or double shot glass), which can lure drinkers into consuming more alcohol than expected.

**Food Slows Absorption.** When estimating BAC levels, consider the amount of food consumed and the length of time between eating and drinking. Food impacts the speed at which alcohol is absorbed into the bloodstream. Alcohol consumed during or after a meal will absorb into the bloodstream at a slower pace, which inevitably delays the effects of intoxication; conversely, drinking on an empty stomach leads to rapid alcohol absorption, which naturally increases the effects of intoxication.

**Rate of Consumption.** The consumption of alcohol at a constant pace will generally result in a more predictable BAC level. In other words, drinking two beers per hour for five hours will create a lower BAC than guzzling ten beers in a couple hours before submitting to a chemical test. Although waiting several hours after the consumption of alcohol is usually better than constant drinking up to the time of driving, there are exceptions to this general rule. For instance, if a chemical test is performed immediately after the rapid consumption of alcohol, the BAC result will be relatively low because the alcohol did not have sufficient time to absorb into the

# Chart 1

## Alcohol Content of Common Beverages

| Beverage Type | % of Alcohol by Volume | Typical Serving Size | Amt. of Alcohol/ Typical Serving |
|---|---|---|---|
| Table Wine | 12 percent | 5 ounces | .60 ounces |
| Wine Cooler | 5 percent | 12 ounces | .60 ounces |
| Regular Beer | 5 percent | 12 ounces | .60 ounces |
| Hard Liquor* | 40 percent | 1¼ ounces | .50 ounces |
| Light Beer | 4 percent | 12 ounces | .48 ounces |

**Note:** Approximate alcohol content in typical servings of common alcoholic beverages. The calculations are an average for all brands. The actual amount of alcohol will vary from brand to brand.

\* Hard liquor represents common brands of vodka, gin, rum, tequila, bourbon, and scotch. Certain name brands may have a higher alcohol content.

---

bloodstream. Thus, it is imperative to monitor individual drinking patterns to reasonably predict BAC levels.

**Biological Factors.** BAC levels are affected by biological influences, such as metabolism, alcohol absorption, stress, and sleep deprivation. These biological factors are silent variables in the BAC equation, and therefore impossible to predict and equally impossible to estimate. Only personal experience can answer this question. Attempt to monitor the amount of alcohol consumed and how it impacts your faculties. Although not a precise science, it offers one more safeguard before driving while intoxicated.

**Beverage Carbonation.** The carbonation level of certain beverages will influence BAC levels by accelerating the rate of alcohol absorption. In other words, a whiskey-sour mixed drink will absorb faster than whiskey and water. Thus, it is advisable to

# Chart 2: Men's BAC Levels Based on Body Weight (pounds) and Hours of Drinking

| lbs. | 120 | | | | 140 | | | | 160 | | | | 180 | | | | 200 | | | | 220 | | | | 240 | | | |
|---|---|---|---|---|---|---|---|---|---|---|---|---|---|---|---|---|---|---|---|---|---|---|---|---|---|---|---|---|
| hrs. | 1 | 2 | 3 | 4 | 1 | 2 | 3 | 4 | 1 | 2 | 3 | 4 | 1 | 2 | 3 | 4 | 1 | 2 | 3 | 4 | 1 | 2 | 3 | 4 | 1 | 2 | 3 | 4 |
| 1 | .02 | .00 | .00 | .00 | .01 | .00 | .00 | .00 | .01 | .00 | .00 | .00 | .00 | .00 | .00 | .00 | .00 | .00 | .00 | .00 | .00 | .00 | .00 | .00 | .00 | .00 | .00 | .00 |
| 2 | .05 | .03 | .01 | .00 | .04 | .02 | .00 | .00 | .03 | .01 | .00 | .00 | .02 | .01 | .00 | .00 | .02 | .00 | .00 | .00 | .02 | .00 | .00 | .00 | .01 | .00 | .00 | .00 |
| 3 | .08 | .06 | .05 | .03 | .06 | .05 | .03 | .01 | .05 | .04 | .02 | .01 | .04 | .03 | .01 | .00 | .04 | .02 | .01 | .00 | .04 | .02 | .00 | .00 | .03 | .01 | .00 | .01 |
| 4 | .11 | .09 | .08 | .06 | .09 | .07 | .06 | .04 | .08 | .06 | .04 | .03 | .06 | .05 | .03 | .02 | .06 | .04 | .02 | .01 | .05 | .04 | .02 | .00 | .04 | .03 | .01 | .03 |
| 5 | .14 | .12 | .11 | .09 | .11 | .10 | .08 | .07 | .10 | .08 | .07 | .05 | .08 | .07 | .06 | .04 | .07 | .06 | .04 | .03 | .07 | .05 | .04 | .02 | .06 | .04 | .03 | .04 |
| 6 | .17 | .15 | .14 | .12 | .14 | .12 | .11 | .09 | .12 | .11 | .09 | .07 | .10 | .09 | .07 | .06 | .09 | .08 | .06 | .04 | .09 | .07 | .05 | .04 | .07 | .06 | .05 | .06 |
| 7 | .20 | .19 | .17 | .15 | .17 | .15 | .13 | .12 | .15 | .13 | .11 | .10 | .12 | .11 | .09 | .08 | .11 | .09 | .08 | .06 | .10 | .09 | .07 | .06 | .09 | .07 | .06 | .04 |
| 8 | .23 | .22 | .20 | .18 | .19 | .18 | .16 | .14 | .17 | .15 | .14 | .12 | .14 | .13 | .11 | .10 | .13 | .11 | .10 | .08 | .12 | .10 | .09 | .07 | .10 | .09 | .07 | .06 |
| 9 | .26 | .25 | .23 | .22 | .22 | .20 | .19 | .17 | .19 | .18 | .16 | .14 | .16 | .15 | .13 | .12 | .15 | .13 | .11 | .10 | .14 | .12 | .11 | .09 | .12 | .10 | .09 | .07 |
| 10 | .29 | .28 | .26 | .25 | .24 | .23 | .21 | .20 | .21 | .20 | .18 | .17 | .18 | .17 | .15 | .14 | .16 | .15 | .13 | .12 | .15 | .14 | .12 | .11 | .13 | .12 | .10 | .09 |
| 11 | .33 | .31 | .29 | .28 | .27 | .25 | .24 | .22 | .24 | .22 | .21 | .19 | .20 | .19 | .17 | .16 | .18 | .17 | .15 | .13 | .17 | .16 | .14 | .12 | .15 | .13 | .12 | .10 |
| 12 | .36 | .34 | .32 | .31 | .30 | .28 | .26 | .25 | .26 | .24 | .23 | .21 | .22 | .21 | .19 | .18 | .20 | .18 | .17 | .15 | .19 | .17 | .16 | .14 | .16 | .15 | .13 | .12 |
| 13 | .39 | .38 | .36 | .34 | .32 | .30 | .29 | .27 | .28 | .27 | .25 | .24 | .24 | .23 | .21 | .20 | .22 | .20 | .19 | .17 | .20 | .19 | .17 | .16 | .18 | .16 | .15 | .13 |
| 14 | .42 | .41 | .39 | .37 | .35 | .33 | .32 | .30 | .30 | .29 | .27 | .26 | .26 | .25 | .23 | .22 | .24 | .22 | .20 | .19 | .22 | .21 | .19 | .17 | .19 | .18 | .16 | .15 |
| 15 | .45 | .44 | .42 | .40 | .37 | .35 | .34 | .33 | .33 | .31 | .30 | .28 | .28 | .27 | .25 | .24 | .25 | .23 | .22 | .21 | .24 | .23 | .21 | .19 | .21 | .19 | .18 | .16 |
| 16 | .48 | .47 | .45 | .43 | .40 | .38 | .37 | .35 | .35 | .34 | .32 | .30 | .30 | .29 | .27 | .26 | .27 | .25 | .23 | .22 | .25 | .24 | .23 | .22 | .22 | .21 | .19 | .18 |

NUMBER OF DRINKS

# Chart 3: Women's BAC Levels Based on Body Weight (pounds) and Hours of Drinking

| NUMBER OF DRINKS | 100 hrs 1 | 2 | 3 | 4 | 120 hrs 1 | 2 | 3 | 4 | 140 hrs 1 | 2 | 3 | 4 | 160 hrs 1 | 2 | 3 | 4 | 180 hrs 1 | 2 | 3 | 4 | 200 hrs 1 | 2 | 3 | 4 | 220 hrs 1 | 2 | 3 | 4 |
|---|---|---|---|---|---|---|---|---|---|---|---|---|---|---|---|---|---|---|---|---|---|---|---|---|---|---|---|---|
| 1 | .03 | .01 | .00 | .00 | .02 | .01 | .00 | .00 | .02 | .00 | .00 | .00 | .01 | .00 | .00 | .00 | .01 | .00 | .00 | .00 | .01 | .00 | .00 | .00 | .00 | .00 | .00 | .00 |
| 2 | .07 | .06 | .04 | .03 | .06 | .04 | .03 | .01 | .05 | .03 | .02 | .00 | .04 | .02 | .01 | .00 | .03 | .02 | .01 | .00 | .03 | .01 | .00 | .00 | .02 | .01 | .00 | .00 |
| 3 | .12 | .10 | .09 | .07 | .10 | .08 | .06 | .05 | .08 | .06 | .05 | .03 | .07 | .05 | .04 | .02 | .06 | .04 | .03 | .01 | .05 | .03 | .02 | .00 | .04 | .03 | .01 | .00 |
| 4 | .16 | .15 | .13 | .12 | .13 | .12 | .10 | .08 | .11 | .10 | .08 | .06 | .10 | .08 | .06 | .05 | .08 | .07 | .05 | .04 | .07 | .06 | .04 | .02 | .06 | .05 | .03 | .02 |
| 5 | .21 | .19 | .18 | .16 | .17 | .15 | .14 | .12 | .14 | .13 | .11 | .10 | .12 | .11 | .09 | .08 | .11 | .09 | .08 | .06 | .09 | .08 | .06 | .05 | .08 | .07 | .05 | .04 |
| 6 | .25 | .24 | .22 | .21 | .21 | .19 | .17 | .16 | .18 | .16 | .14 | .13 | .15 | .14 | .12 | .10 | .13 | .12 | .10 | .09 | .12 | .10 | .08 | .07 | .10 | .09 | .07 | .06 |
| 7 | .30 | .28 | .27 | .25 | .24 | .22 | .21 | .20 | .21 | .19 | .18 | .16 | .18 | .16 | .15 | .13 | .16 | .14 | .13 | .11 | .14 | .12 | .11 | .09 | .12 | .11 | .09 | .08 |
| 8 | .34 | .33 | .31 | .30 | .28 | .26 | .25 | .23 | .24 | .22 | .21 | .19 | .21 | .19 | .18 | .16 | .18 | .17 | .15 | .13 | .16 | .14 | .13 | .11 | .14 | .13 | .11 | .10 |
| 9 | .39 | .37 | .36 | .34 | .32 | .30 | .29 | .27 | .27 | .26 | .24 | .22 | .24 | .21 | .20 | .19 | .21 | .19 | .18 | .16 | .18 | .17 | .15 | .13 | .16 | .15 | .13 | .12 |
| 10 | .43 | .42 | .40 | .39 | .35 | .33 | .32 | .31 | .30 | .29 | .27 | .26 | .26 | .25 | .23 | .22 | .23 | .22 | .20 | .19 | .20 | .19 | .17 | .16 | .18 | .17 | .15 | .14 |
| 11 | .48 | .46 | .45 | .43 | .39 | .37 | .36 | .34 | .34 | .32 | .30 | .29 | .29 | .28 | .26 | .24 | .26 | .24 | .23 | .21 | .23 | .21 | .19 | .18 | .20 | .19 | .17 | .16 |
| 12 | .52 | .51 | .49 | .48 | .43 | .41 | .40 | .38 | .37 | .35 | .34 | .32 | .32 | .30 | .29 | .27 | .28 | .27 | .25 | .24 | .25 | .23 | .22 | .20 | .22 | .21 | .19 | .18 |
| 13 | .57 | .55 | .54 | .52 | .46 | .44 | .43 | .42 | .40 | .38 | .37 | .35 | .35 | .33 | .32 | .30 | .31 | .29 | .28 | .26 | .27 | .25 | .24 | .22 | .24 | .23 | .21 | .20 |
| 14 | .61 | .60 | .58 | .57 | .50 | .48 | .47 | .45 | .43 | .42 | .40 | .38 | .38 | .36 | .34 | .33 | .33 | .32 | .30 | .29 | .29 | .27 | .26 | .24 | .26 | .25 | .23 | .22 |
| 15 | .66 | .64 | .63 | .61 | .54 | .52 | .51 | .49 | .46 | .45 | .43 | .42 | .41 | .39 | .37 | .36 | .36 | .34 | .33 | .31 | .31 | .29 | .28 | .27 | .28 | .27 | .25 | .24 |
| 16 | .70 | .69 | .68 | .66 | .57 | .55 | .54 | .53 | .50 | .48 | .46 | .45 | .43 | .42 | .40 | .38 | .38 | .37 | .35 | .34 | .33 | .32 | .30 | .29 | .30 | .29 | .27 | .26 |

mix alcohol with water or fruit juices to more accurately predict BAC levels.

**Medication and Drugs.** Avoid mixing alcohol and drugs, regardless of whether it is over-the-counter, by prescription, or illegal. It is unlawful to operate a motor vehicle if the drug, either alone or in conjunction with alcohol, impairs driving abilities. Although there are legal exceptions to this general rule, consult a pharmacist to determine whether mixing alcohol and medications will cause driving impairment.

# Establishing Intoxication

When prosecuting a drunk driving charge, every state uses objective and subjective tests to establish intoxication. Although the subjective test is easiest to refute, it is important to understand the theories, as well as the limitations, behind both methods of testing.

**Objective Test.** The objective method estimates BAC levels using scientific and medical evidence that analyzes body specimens of blood, breath or urine. Although the reliability of chemical testing is contingent upon many variables, the breath result is considered least reliable, whereas the blood test is most credible.

There are numerous factors that affect the reliability of chemical test results. Each test involves a series of calculations using scientific theories based upon the average person. Since the tests fail to consider individual characteristics and physiological factors, the results may not accurately reflect BAC levels. Moreover, the tests fail to consider tolerance levels. Some individuals can have near-toxic BAC levels, yet fail to exhibit many of the negative effects associated with excessive alcohol consumption.

**Subjective Test.** The subjective test utilizes individual senses to identify intoxicated behavior. In most instances, this involves a police officer trained in detecting the indicators of intoxication, i.e., bloodshot/watery eyes, smell of alcohol, unsteady balance, flushed face, slurred speech, and either despondent or excited behavior. Since the subjective test incorporates human fallibility, the evidence is easier to refute using logical explanations for the seemingly intoxicated behavior.

**BAC Level When Driving.** When prosecuting a drunk driving case, the state must prove the motorist was legally intoxicated at the time of driving. Naturally, any time lapse between driving and the chemical test can significantly alter the accuracy of a BAC result. In fact, many states restrict the admissibility of chemical testing evidence acquired two hours after the alleged driving.

Similarly, the accuracy of BAC results is questionable when alcohol is consumed *after* the driving occurred. Even if a chemical test indicates a BAC above the legal limit, the result would include alcohol consumed after the driving ceased. In other words, consuming alcohol after driving makes it very difficult to convict because prosecutors cannot prove the defendant was legally intoxicated at the time of driving.

# Drug/Medication Usage

The other means of prosecuting motorists for drunk driving is the operation of a motor vehicle while under the influence of drugs or a combination of drugs and alcohol. If a person is taking prescription medication under the direction of a licensed physician, and the operation of a motor vehicle is not restricted, then a person may lawfully drive. However, in the absence of a prescription, using an illegal substance, or engaging in unauthorized driving, a motorist can be prosecuted for drunk driving. This rule also applies to over-the-counter drugs.

**Legal Definition.** Despite sparse case law outlining the definition of drug, most statutes only mandate that the substance impairs driving abilities to *any* extent. If a motorist is buzzing from a sugar high, theoretically, the state could prosecute the person for drunk driving. In fact, a person has been convicted for using lawfully prescribed insulin.

**Consult a Pharmacist.** Always consult a physician or pharmacist regarding the safe operation of a motor vehicle and whether certain medications cause an adverse reaction when mixed with alcohol. A warning or reasonable belief not to consume alcohol when driving is sufficient for a drunk driving conviction.

**Subjective Drug Testing.** There are eight field sobriety tests to determine drug use: horizontal gaze nystagmus (HGN), pupil reaction, pupil size, standing steadiness, one-leg stand, walk-the-line, finger-to-nose, and pulse rate. Officers may also consider skin marks, apathy, drowsiness, and hyperactivity. Although relatively accurate indicators of drug use, the reliability of individual results is contingent upon the training and experience of the officer administering the tests.

# Chapter Two

# State Laws

---

# Crime and Punishment

State lawmakers assume that motorists do not realize the dangers of drinking and driving so they repeatedly enact stringent legislation designed to protect society and punish offenders. Although advocates of harsh drunk driving laws promote the benefits of education, in reality, the system is punitive and devoid of effective methods of reducing the number of repeat offenders.

For a conviction, most drunk driving statutes require proof that the motorist is either operating a motor vehicle under the influence of alcohol or drugs, or has a blood-alcohol concentration (BAC) at or above the legal limit. "Under the influence" is often defined as a motorist exhibiting one or more of the following characteristics: 1) affected reason or mental ability; 2) impaired judgment; 3) visibly excited emotions; or 4) losing control of bodily actions or motions so that the ability to safely operate a motor vehicle is diminished to any extent.

# Punishment and Sanctions

Drunk driving laws impose dual punishment: criminal (jail sentence and fines) and civil (driver's license suspension). The criminal penalty often escalates with each offense or aggravating circumstance, such as damage to property, serious personal injury, or death. The civil sanction is based upon similar factors, as well as evidence of a chemical test, driving history, and age of the motorist. When a minor is involved, many states impose harsher driver's license sanctions despite registering a *lower* BAC result.

# Criminal Punishment

The severity of criminal punishment varies from state to state, and escalates with each prior drunk driving conviction. The level of offense is usually determined by the number of years between conviction and the date of the next offense, regardless of whether a deferred judgment was received. Most states count all prior drunk driving offenses, even when it occurred in a different state (but only if the statute is comparable). To determine the number of years each state uses to enhance the criminal penalty, purchase a copy of *Drunk Driving Laws: Rules of the Road When Crossing State Lines*, which summarizes the laws of every state. For instance, Colorado and Wisconsin have a 5-year penalty-enhancement period, while Vermont enhances the offense up to 15 years after the second drunk driving conviction.

**Calculating Penalty-Enhancement Period.** When calculating the level of offense, consider the following illustration according to Wisconsin's 5-year penalty-enhancement statute. If convicted on January 1, 1998 and accused of drunk driving on December 31, 2002, the motorist will be charged with second offense drunk driving (even if the conviction does not go on record until July 1, 2003). The period of enhancement is measured from the date of conviction to the date of the next alleged criminal act.

In another scenario involving Wisconsin law, if a motorist is convicted on January 1, 1998, convicted on January 1, 2001, and accused of drunk driving on January 2, 2003, the motorist will be charged with second offense drunk driving. It is not a third offense because more than 5 years lapsed between the date of the first conviction and the date of the alleged third drunk driving incident (i.e., 5 years and one day).

Moreover, the severity of imprisonment and fines vary from state to state. It is essential to purchase a copy of *Drunk Driving Laws: Rules of the Road When Crossing State Lines* to confirm the statutory punishment in your jurisdiction. There can be a grave disparity between jurisdictions, so know your rights, and the consequences, prior to operating a motor vehicle.

**First Offense.** Criminal punishment varies from state to state. Many states range from a minimum number of hours in jail and a standard fine to a maximum jail sentence and heftier fine. This gives the judge sentencing discretion to severely punish defendants with a negative criminal history. If a jail sentence is imposed, the court can often grant work release or order that the sentence be served on weekends. Some jurisdictions waive the fine under certain circumstances (e.g., no injury to person or property), or the court can grant a deferred judgment. In lieu of a fine, the court will sometimes order unpaid community service. A substance abuse evaluation is usually required prior to the sentencing hearing, and the court typically orders the motorist to attend a drunk driving class.

**Second Offense.** A second offense drunk driving conviction has a longer mandatory jail sentence and a higher minimum fine. Some jurisdictions require the jail term to be served on consecutive days unless undue hardship exists. There is also a discretionary range of punishment for the judge to consider with a maximum jail sentence and a sizeable fine. In some jurisdictions, a deferred judgment or suspended sentence is still available. A substance abuse evaluation is usually required, and the court will order completion of all recommended treatment.

**Third or Subsequent Offense.** A third or subsequent drunk driving offense usually results in a felony conviction and an exorbitant fine. In some jurisdictions, the jail sentence must be served on consecutive days unless the defendant can show undue hardship, and most defendants must undergo substance abuse treatment in a residential treatment facility.

**Serious Injury to Others.** If the drunk driving incident results in serious injury to others, the maximum punishment is usually five years in prison, and the defendant is usually barred from obtaining a deferred judgment.

**Death to Others.** If the drunk driving incident results in a death, the maximum punishment can be 25 years in prison. In most circumstances, the defendant is not entitled to a deferred judgment.

**Penalties for Minors.** Persons under the age of 21 are subject to the same criminal punishment as motorists who have reached the age of majority.

# Substance Abuse Evaluation

In most drunk driving arrests, the motorist is placed in jail and has an initial appearance with a judge the following morning. At this hearing the judge often orders the defendant to obtain a substance abuse evaluation. The purpose of the evaluation is to determine whether the defendant has a substance abuse problem.

Unfortunately, this seemingly innocuous report will heavily influence the prosecutor's recommendation, the defense attorney's options, and the court's punishment. Since the evaluation is so critical, defendants should properly prepare their responses with the same degree of seriousness.

# Restitution

The court generally orders the defendant to pay restitution to victims, which is credited toward any future civil judgment. Evidence in a restitution proceeding is not admissible in a subsequent civil trial. The prosecuting attorney is often required to file a statement of pecuniary damages to outline restitution costs within 30 days of the sentencing hearing.

# Chapter Three

# Driving Privileges

# Penalties and Sanctions

Most states adhere to the precept that driving is a privilege, not a fundamental right, so any driver's license sanction is considered remedial, not punitive. In the drunk driving context, this means that a criminal charge is separate and distinct from a driver's license suspension. In other words, an acquittal on a drunk driving charge has no bearing on the department of transportation's ability to lawfully suspend driving privileges based upon the drunk driving charge.

The seemingly illogical consequence is predicated on the legal definition of punishment. The criminal charge is punishment because a jail term can be imposed; whereas, a driver's license suspension is remedial because no incarceration can occur. Furthermore, the standard of proof is different. In a criminal case, the state must prove guilt beyond a reasonable doubt; in a civil case, the legal standard is a preponderance of the evidence (i.e., more likely than not).

# Notice of Suspension

The driver's license suspension period typically begins ten days after receiving notice of the suspension, either by certified mail from the department of transportation (DOT) or verbally from the officer at the time of a chemical test failure or refusal. The officer will usually serve notice, confiscate the driver's license, issue a 10-day permit, and forward the license to the department of transportation. This allows the motorist adequate time to request a hearing to challenge the legitimacy of any suspension.

# Driver's License Suspension Hearing

In most driver's license suspension hearings, the motorist must contest the sanction by requesting a hearing within ten days after receiving notice of the suspension. The hearing is held by an administrative law judge (ALJ) who determines whether the officer had reasonable grounds to believe the motorist was operating a vehicle in violation of the drunk driving laws. The ALJ will either rescind or sustain the suspension. The motorist can appeal the decision to the director of driver services, who will either rescind or sustain the suspension, or order a new hearing. Usually the motorist is allowed to drive during the pendency of these administrative proceedings; however, this does not always apply to minors.

Besides delaying the suspension period, another benefit of requesting a hearing is to acquire valuable information. Although an attorney is not required to participate in the administrative proceeding, counsel can protect and preserve certain legal rights for the criminal trial. In effect, the DOT hearing functions as an inexpensive deposition to highlight the strengths and weaknesses of a case. Moreover, the information is acquired before the prosecuting attorney has time to prepare. The DOT is often represented by an inexperienced law school intern, so defense lawyers can often unearth crucial evidence to bolster their case.

Since the driver's license suspension hearing is usually audio recorded, defense counsel can obtain a copy of the record for future litigation. The transcript is not only useful for investigating the case and preparing for depositions, but also discrediting the officer's testimony at trial. Illuminating an officer's falsehood or contradictory testimony is often the difference between winning and losing a case.

# Length of Suspension

The length of a driver's license suspension is contingent upon many factors--test result or refusal, BAC level, prior driving record and severity of offenses, number and length of time between prior drunk driving incidents, and the defendant's age. Since each state has different rules and regulations governing driver's license suspensions in the drunk driving context, it is imperative to purchase *Drunk Driving Laws: Rules of the Road When Crossing State Lines* for an accurate overview of each state's drunk driving laws.

**Serious Injury to Others.** If the motorist is involved in a personal injury accident, the court usually determines whether the consumption of alcohol resulted in serious injury to anyone other than the driver. If so, the court can often suspend driving privileges and limit eligibility for a temporary restricted license (TRL).

**Death to Others.** When a drunk driving accident causes a death, many jurisdictions suspend driving privileges for six years and deny a TRL for at least two years. In addition, the defendant is often required to attend a drunk driving course, obtain a substance abuse evaluation, and complete all recommended treatment.

**Driving Under Suspension.** Operating a motor vehicle while driving privileges are suspended is a serious criminal offense. In addition to criminal penalties, the defendant receives a lengthier driver's license suspension and all TRL privileges are rescinded.

# Temporary Restricted License (TRL)

A temporary restricted license (TRL), often termed a work permit, only authorizes motorists to use a motor vehicle for limited purposes. In most states, a drunk driving arrest or conviction does not prevent the motorist from obtaining a TRL.

**Authorized Uses.** A TRL can only be used to travel from home to specified places that are verifiable by the department of transportation. Appropriate uses include: full or part-time employment; continuing health care of self or dependent persons; continuing education while pursuing a diploma, degree or certification; substance abuse treatment; or court-ordered community service. A TRL cannot be used for pleasure driving.

**Eligibility Requirements.** Before an applicant is eligible for a TRL, most states have statutory requirements that must be satisfied: 1) the applicant has only one prior drunk driving suspension within the penalty-enhancement period; 2) their license is not under suspension for any other reason; 3) the hard suspension period has elapsed; 4) vehicles are appropriately insured; and 5) installation of an ignition interlock device in all vehicles.

**Other Motorists.** A minor is often ineligible for a TRL when the driver's license suspension results from a drunk driving offense. Motorists possessing a commercial vehicle license are ineligible for a TRL when the drunk driving incident involves the operation of a commercial vehicle. Finally, a TRL does not allow anyone to operate a school bus.

# Ignition Interlock Device (IID)

To remain eligible for a temporary restricted license, many jurisdictions require the installation of an ignition interlock device (IID) in all vehicles operated by the defendant. The IID is a mechanism connected to the vehicle's ignition that measures ethanol within a person's breath. When a driver blows into the device and the ethanol concentration exceeds a pre-programmed BAC level, the vehicle's ignition will not function. Some IIDs require constant monitoring of breath-ethanol levels during vehicle operation. The IID is usually installed for the entire length of the driver's license suspension period. Failure to install the IID can result in contempt of court, and tampering with the device is a criminal offense punishable by jail or fine.

# License Reinstatement

After driving privileges are suspended, the defendant is usually required to attend a state-approved drunk driving course. In some jurisdictions, the defendant is required to obtain a substance abuse evaluation, treatment, or rehabilitation services. Driving privileges are not reinstated until the defendant offers proof of completion and pays all applicable costs.

# Vehicle Impoundment/Immobilization

Impoundment is where the police take temporary physical possession of a motor vehicle to prevent operation by the owner. Immobilization is where the police render the vehicle inoperable by installing a club on the steering wheel. Immobilization is considerably less expensive than impoundment because there are no storage fees; however, the judge often has discretion to impose either sanction.

**First Offense.** There is usually no impoundment or immobilization issue for first offense drunk driving convictions.

**Second or Subsequent Offense.** Impoundment or immobilization of a motor vehicle is a common occurrence for a second or subsequent drunk driving offense. Operating or selling a vehicle subject to an impoundment or immobilization order is a crime, which can often result in seizure and forfeiture of the vehicle. Similarly, the owner of an impounded or immobilized vehicle is subject to criminal charges and joint civil liability for allowing the defendant to drive their vehicle subject to an impoundment/immobilization order.

Fortunately, there is a legal loophole. If the vehicle title is transferred into the name of a third party prior to a sentencing hearing, the law does not apply. The court cannot order impoundment or immobilization if the vehicle is no longer owned by someone directly associated with the drunk driving offense. Furthermore, certain individuals are allowed to drive an impounded or immobilized vehicle. It usually requires a court order, proof that the applicant's driving privileges are not suspended, and installation of an ignition interlock device. Consult with an attorney for the exceptions.

---

# Chapter Four

# Vehicle Stops

---

# Police Conduct

In most vehicle stops initiated by a police officer, the motorist experiences anxiety. This condition is often exacerbated at night because some officers believe that every motorist on the road between 10:00 p.m. and 5:00 a.m. is a drunk driver. Some officers require every driver to perform field sobriety tests, regardless of whether the officer has any evidence of alcohol consumption. The purpose of this chapter is to inform motorists of their legal rights and the limitations on police power.

## Legal Standard

Most courts are expanding the legal authority of police officers and restricting the individual rights of defendants. Currently, officers have broad discretion to perform their duties and engage in activity that was previously forbidden. At some point the courts will pull the reins, but the near future appears bleak with respect to protecting defendants' constitutional rights and the privacy interests of motorists.

**Probable Cause.** To initiate a vehicle stop, police officers must have probable cause that criminal activity (e.g., traffic violation) is afoot. However, the current trend of legal precedent is giving officers authority to implement road blocks so officers can indiscriminately interrogate motorists, perform random checks of vehicle license plates, or stop vehicles for engaging in *lawful* driving behavior, such as weaving within the lane. Probable cause can be generated by the officer's innocent observations. For instance, a motorist has a reasonable expectation of privacy while the vehicle is moving, but the interior is not protected from visual observations by an officer while the vehicle is stopped or parked.

**Suppressing Evidence.** When a police officer lacks probable cause for a police stop, the defendant can petition the court to suppress the evidence. A police officer's mere suspicion of criminal activity is insufficient to institute a vehicle stop. Similarly, a police officer cannot request a field sobriety test without first establishing probable cause that the motorist was operating a motor vehicle while intoxicated. Since field sobriety tests are considered constitutional searches and perceived as more intrusive than chemical testing, the officer must have sufficient grounds before asking the motorist to perform any field sobriety tests. If adequate grounds are lacking, the evidence will be suppressed and held inadmissible at trial.

# Vehicle Search

Vehicle searches may become an issue if the occupants possess illegal substances or other contraband. Although this may seem irrelevant, it is important to understand the rights of all parties to prepare for the unexpected.

**Vehicle Compartments.** Police officers have vast authority to search vehicles. They can view the interior but their actions are limited upon entering the vehicle. The trunk and glove box are given greater constitutional protection because both are enclosed compartments. Nevertheless, if the vehicle is impounded, officers are usually allowed to search the vehicle to inventory its contents.

**Non-vehicle Containers.** Greater constitutional protection is afforded to enclosed containers that are private possessions of the occupants (purse or briefcase), and not part of the vehicle construction (glove box or trunk). Passengers can refuse a police officer's request to search non-vehicle containers. Even after an arrest, officers usually need a court order to search non-vehicle containers. Although highly private and personal containers receive the most constitutional protection, other items have a lesser degree of privacy, e.g., cardboard box, plastic bag, or suitcase. Since the level of constitutional protection varies with the facts and circumstances of each case, always remember that most containers have some constitutional protection.

# Rights of Occupants

The constitutional rights of vehicle occupants are contingent upon many factors--facts and circumstances of each case, knowledge of illegal activity, and level of control over the vehicle or its contents. In the drunk driving context, the vehicle owner is often concerned about illegal substances or impoundment issues. The driver must be wary of items contained in the vehicle, and the passengers are typically concerned about items in their possession or within the immediate vicinity.

**Vehicle Owner.** If the vehicle owner is not present at the time illegal contraband is discovered, the vehicle occupants are often held accountable. Nevertheless, the owner could face criminal charges if the illegal substance is locked in a container or hidden in a compartment that is not accessible to the vehicle occupants. In certain circumstances, the owner can be held criminally responsible for another motorist's drunk driving incident. Typically, the owner must have knowledge of a prior drunk driving conviction and be aware that the driver would consume alcohol while operating the vehicle.

**Vehicle Driver.** Drivers are most accountable because they have actual physical control of the vehicle. However, other factors influence culpability--physical proximity to the contraband, whether it is located in a locked compartment, and less credible indicators, such as appearance, demeanor, or criminal history. Although the driver often takes most of the responsibility, prosecutors typically have a difficult time gaining a conviction because they cannot prove who had possession of the illegal substance.

**Vehicle Passenger.** The passenger in a vehicle is afforded the greatest constitutional protection. Since the passenger is often a captive occupant who lacks control over their ultimate destination, criminal charges are rarely filed unless the contraband is located in their actual possession. Lack of control over the vehicle is an essential component when evaluating passenger rights.

# Post-Arrest Procedures

After an arrest and being taken to the police station, the motorist is fingerprinted, booked, given a standard-issue jumpsuit, and placed in a holding cell until the initial appearance (usually in the morning). The purpose of an initial appearance is to notify the defendant of all charges, and either set bond or order release from jail without bond. In some instances, instead of spending a night in jail, the officer imposes a standard bond fee that allows the motorist to be immediately released into the custody of a sober caretaker. This is entirely discretionary, and contingent upon jail overcrowding, police policy, defendant cooperation, and the officer's disposition. If released, a court date is set for the initial appearance.

A drunk driving arrest is merely the allegation that criminal activity has occurred--it is not a formal criminal charge. The charge becomes formal upon indictment or the prosecuting attorney filing appropriate papers. There are deadlines for filing formal charges, and in some circumstances the complaint is dismissed. There is often a delay between arrest and indictment to allow the officer time to prepare an official report that substantiates the criminal complaint. This also allows the defendant adequate time to retain an attorney.

# Money Buys Justice

As mentioned earlier, money is a crucial factor in winning a high percentage of drunk driving cases. Large financial reserves allow defense attorneys to pursue all avenues of investigation, discovery and legal representation. Conversely, financial limitations place constraints on the level of justice received. Money buys information, which is the key to winning drunk driving cases. It is not necessary to catch the officer in a lie, nor is it essential to have verifiable proof of sobriety. Instead, the defense attorney must provide competent, credible evidence to convince the jury to vote for an acquittal.

# Chapter Five

# Proving Intoxication

---

# Sensory Indicators

To substantiate a drunk driving arrest, police officers analyze several sensory observations, such as physical coordination, speech pattern, appearance and demeanor. Although it is debatable whether the observations are valid indicators of intoxication, most officers make the first crucial error by equating intoxication with a late-night traffic violation. Inevitably, the officer will have a skewed perception of the motorist's sobriety prior to speaking with the driver. The purpose of this chapter is to offer insight into motorists' rights when officers attempt to prove intoxication using sensory observations.

## Driving Behavior

In most drunk driving arrests the defendant is accused of operating a motor vehicle in a manner consistent with alcohol impairment. Although driving errors often occur without the presence of alcohol, many jurors will believe the officer unless contrary evidence is presented. A typical drunk driving arrest involves a minor traffic infraction, such as speeding, failing to come

# Chart 4
# Detecting Drunk Drivers at Night

| | |
|---|---|
| Straddling center or lane marker | 65 |
| Turning with wide radius | 65 |
| Weaving | 60 |
| Almost striking object or vehicle | 60 |
| Appearing to be drunk | 60 |
| Swerving | 55 |
| Driving on other than designated roadway | 55 |
| Drifting | 50 |
| Stopping (without cause) in traffic lane | 50 |
| Slow speed (more than 10 m.p.h. below limit) | 50 |
| Driving into opposing or crossing traffic | 45 |
| Braking erratically | 45 |
| Tires on center or lane marker | 45 |
| Following too close | 45 |
| Signaling inconsistent with driving actions | 40 |
| Turning abruptly or illegally | 35 |
| Stopping inappropriately (other than in lane) | 35 |
| Headlights off | 30 |
| Accelerating or decelerating rapidly | 30 |

**Note:** Indicates the chances out of 100 that a driver's BAC is .10 or higher.

---

to a complete stop, or weaving in the lane. However, each law violation has a logical explanation that is unrelated to alcohol intake or impairment, i.e., being in a hurry, having unaligned wheels, or driving on an irregular road surface.

The National Highway Traffic Safety Administration (NHTSA) conducted a study of various driving infractions that are often associated with drunk driving. (*See* Chart 4). Jurors are often shocked to discover that 40 out of 100 drivers who "appear to be drunk" to police officers, are in fact, not under the influence. Similarly, 40 out of 100 drivers who nearly strike another vehicle are legally sober. The NHTSA study also calculates the likelihood of driver intoxication when multiple infractions occur. When two or more infractions are present, add 10 to the highest value among all the infractions observed. For example, if the subject is turning with a wide radius (65), breaking erratically (45), and turning abruptly (35), there is a 75% chance the driver has a BAC of .10 or more.

# Appearance and Demeanor

It is common knowledge that the indicators of intoxication are fatally flawed because sober individuals are often characterized as being intoxicated. According to the United States legislature, there are approximately 60 pathological conditions that exhibit symptoms of alcohol consumption. Moreover, alcohol symptoms may be the product of illness or medication, insulin overdose or deficiency, nervous system injuries, concussions, or hypoglycemia.

Nevertheless, officers are adamant that their sensory observations definitively prove intoxication. The following is a list of the most frequently cited activities that police officers claim are indicators of intoxicated behavior:

1) odor of alcohol
2) bloodshot, watery or glassy eyes
3) slurred or thick speech
4) flushed complexion
5) staggering and stumbling
6) fumbling with wallet
7) clothing in disarray or poor grooming
8) rambling or despondent

Naturally, there are reasonable, legitimate, and sober explanations for the alleged "intoxicated" behavior.

**Smell of Alcohol.** The smell of alcohol is actually the flavoring of most alcoholic beverages. Beer and wine have significantly stronger odors than hard liquor. However, the odor has no correlation to the amount of alcohol consumed. Furthermore, certain illnesses create comparable breath odors, and belching causes gaseous odors to remain in the throat for ten minutes.

**Bloodshot Eyes.** There are numerous explanations for bloodshot eyes: 1) fatigue or insomnia; 2) environmental conditions (dust, heat or wind); 3) normal eye condition; 4) eye irritation from a foreign object; 5) old or dirty contact lenses; 6) air pollution; 7) allergies; 8) extensive reading; or 9) prolonged eye strain.

**Slurred Speech.** This fallacious indicator of intoxication is misleading because a police officer rarely knows the defendant's regular speech pattern. Some individuals talk slowly or have speech impediments, which are valid explanations for thick or slurred speech. Moreover, cold weather numbs facial muscles and causes pronunciation problems.

**Flushed Face.** It is not uncommon for people to have a natural rosy complexion, especially with older persons, or to become flushed during the anxiety and embarrassment of a police stop. Since the officer often lacks any prior contact with the driver, these are legitimate explanations. Moreover, reddish hues can be the product of medication, excessive makeup, extreme weather conditions, either hot, humid days or windburn from cold weather.

**Coordination.** Several acts of incoordination are perceived as proof of intoxication. However, most miscues have reasonable explanations, such as nervousness, inclement weather, or stiff joints

---

after exiting the vehicle. There are other legitimate explanations, 1) medical condition, e.g., back, leg, foot, or inner ear disorder; 2) shoe type; 3) sole imperfections; or 4) uneven road surface.

**Poor Grooming.** Officers often equate unkempt appearance with intoxication. Although this may be true in some circumstances, typically the reason is related to other factors: natural wrinkle in clothes, wearing work clothes from a dirty environment, wearing sweatpants or sweatshirt for comfort, or wearing ragged clothes as a fashion statement. In addition, uncombed hair can occur on a windy day; and facial hair may be the product of rapid hair growth, personal preference, or overly sensitive skin that prohibits daily shaving.

**Rambling or Despondency.** According to police officers, a talkative disposition indicates alcohol impairment because the defendant is visibly excited; however, melancholy is also evidence of intoxication because alcohol is a depressant. In reality, neither behavior is evidence of intoxication unless there is additional evidence of the person's normal behavior.

# Chapter Six

# Sobriety Tests

---

# Subjective Fallibility

Few motorists know their legal rights when approached by a police officer at the scene of a vehicle stop. Although officers have considerable authoritative discretion, motorists have some constitutional rights that must be honored. Police officers have power to control the movement of vehicle occupants, but there is a thin line between lawful conduct and unconstitutional police action. Since motorists' rights vary with the circumstances, this chapter offers some of the constitutional theories behind common factual scenarios.

## Police Stop

In a typical drunk driving incident, the police officer approaches the vehicle to communicate with the motorist. The officer also begins observing the driver, passenger(s), and vehicle contents, which often includes sniffing the vehicle interior, as well as monitoring the driver's appearance and demeanor. If the officer asks whether alcohol was consumed, the answer often has similar consequences--a denial will result in the officer ordering the driver to perform field sobriety tests, whereas an admission will still result in field sobriety tests. In either scenario, the officer will use all incriminating evidence against the defendant at trial. Since officers are duty-bound to arrest individuals suspected of criminal conduct, motorists rarely talk their way out of a drunk driving charge. As a general rule, everything uttered at the scene of the police stop will be used against the motorist in a court of law, even if the officer never read the Miranda advisement.

# Field Sobriety Tests - Generally

Police officers are trained to administer three nationally standardized field sobriety tests--horizontal gaze nystagmus (HGN), walk-the-line, and one-leg stand. The tests presumably measure intoxication through divided-attention activities (combination of mental and physical activities) or involuntary responses. The divided-attention activities include the one-leg lift (counting to 30 while holding one leg in the air), and walk-the-line (counting nine steps while walking heel-to-toe, then turning around and repeating the same activity). The involuntary response test, or HGN, measures eye movement to assess intoxication.

**Subjectivity.** The most pivotal flaw in field sobriety tests is a lack of scientific objectivity. The results of each standardized test is based upon the officer's biased sensory observations. By simply requesting a motorist to perform field sobriety tests, the officer is exhibiting a conscious or subconscious preconception that the driver is impaired. Inevitably, common human behaviors are misconstrued as evidence of intoxication. Thus, never attempt to impress the officer with evidence of sobriety. Listen to the directions closely, and follow them precisely. Any deviation will be construed as a test failure.

**Reliability and Accuracy.** The one-leg stand is 65% accurate, while the walk-the-line test is 68% accurate. Even the HGN has a reliability rate of only 77%. When all three tests are performed and scored, the combined accuracy in predicting legal intoxication is 83.4%.

# Divided-Attention Tests

There are numerous limitations to the accuracy of divided-attention field sobriety tests. The operation of a motor vehicle involves a divided-attention activity. In other words, if the motorist is stopped for a defective headlight, and not erratic driving, this is evidence that the motorist was capable of performing a more difficult divided-attention test. Furthermore, a NHTSA study indicates that most minor traffic infractions do not constitute evidence of intoxication. (*See* Chart 4).

**Accuracy.** Divided-attention field sobriety tests lack credibility because the accuracy rate varies with environmental conditions. The one-leg lift should be performed on a smooth, level surface, but is often administered at the scene of a traffic stop on an irregular or rough surface, which can affect balance. The walk-the-line test should be performed with adequate lighting and straight lines to guide walking, but usually are administered at night using cracks in the road surface.

Both tests are further flawed when executed by individuals at least 50 pounds overweight, over 60 years of age, having physical conditions that affect balance (leg, back, or inner ear disorder), or persons with only one functional eye or other depth perception problems.

**Inherent Flaws.** The problem with field sobriety test accuracy is that results rely upon subjective human evaluations, when there are numerous external factors that influence individual performance, such as mental or physical condition, testing environment, or officer prejudice. Physical tests are influenced by weather, shoe type, age, physical limitations, illness, nervousness, or anger. Caffeine even distorts test results, and the combination of alcohol and caffeine affects muscular coordination and accurate timing. Another contributing factor is the circadian rhythm, which involves the 24-hour biological clock in humans. Persons are more likely to perform poorly on field sobriety tests during the early morning hours or while experiencing jet lag.

# Involuntary Field Sobriety Tests

The horizontal gaze nystagmus (HGN) involves monitoring the eyes while they follow a moving object, usually the tip of a pen. The pen is approximately six inches from the nose, and slowly moved toward each shoulder and then toward the forehead and chest. If the eyes begin jerking, as opposed to smooth movement, before the pen reaches a 45-degree angle, this is supposed to indicate alcohol impairment.

Although the HGN measures an involuntary physical response, its accuracy requires adequate lighting and precise measuring devices. In most drunk driving arrests, the test is performed on a dark street with the officer estimating a 45-degree angle. Unfortunately, the test results are unreliable at 55-degrees. The presence of chemicals or drugs, such as barbiturates, antihistamines, phencyclidine, depressants, anticonvulsants, caffeine, nicotine or aspirin can cause nystagmus (jerking of the eyes). Even atmospheric pressure, biological ailments, or fatigued eyes, either from prolonged use or inadequate lighting, can cause nystagmus.

# Non-standardized Field Sobriety Tests

Besides the NHTSA tests, sometimes officers administer non-standardized physical and verbal field sobriety tests to measure intoxication. Physical tests measure balance, while verbal tests measure mental acuity. Although officers typically administer the NHTSA field sobriety tests, nontraditional sobriety tests may be used to supplement the standardized routine.

**Physical Tests.** There are several physical performance field sobriety tests that measure coordination. The most common is standing at attention for 30 seconds to monitor body sway. This test is unreliable because alcohol does not significantly affect body sway until nearly three hours after the cessation of drinking. Another common test is picking up coins from the ground to measure eye-hand coordination and balance. Occasionally, the officer will request the motorist to write the alphabet. In theory, intoxication causes sloppy penmanship; in reality, it could be the product of speed, nervousness, or the type of writing utensil.

**Verbal Tests.** There are several verbal field sobriety tests, and the most common is reciting the alphabet (without singing the song). A more challenging, if not impossible test, is reciting the alphabet backwards. Another verbal test is counting backwards between two designated numbers. In these tests, an improper response could be the product of mental deficiency, inadequate education, or attempting to impress the officer with an exhibition of sobriety.

# Right to Refuse Field Sobriety Tests

Motorists have the right to refuse an officer's request for field sobriety tests (FSTs). There is no legal requirement that a driver must perform FSTs before or after an arrest. An officer can only request, not compel, a motorist to perform the tests. The critical issue, which has yet to be resolved by the courts, is whether the refusal to perform FSTs is admissible evidence to prove intoxication. Thus, it is imperative that a motion to suppress is filed because otherwise the issue may not be properly preserved for appeal.

# Miranda Rights

In drunk driving cases, the Miranda advisement is sometimes useful for excluding incriminating evidence at trial. The advisement is a legal duty imposed upon officers to inform defendants of their right to remain silent, have an attorney present, and avoid self-incrimination. The advisement is only important if the motorist provides harmful statements *after* the arrest. However, most conversations and field sobriety tests at the scene of a vehicle stop are considered pre-arrest activities, and therefore admissible evidence.

Often officers use a detailed questionnaire to acquire information about the defendant. According to the law, officers are allowed to gather physical evidence, not testimonial evidence. Thus, an appropriate inquiry would involve the defendant's preferences, while an improper subject would include the time of day, current location, day of the week, etc. The latter is testimonial evidence and subject to suppression. In many drunk driving cases the officer fails to recite Miranda rights, which may be important to suppress potentially damaging evidence.

# Drugs/Medication

The NHTSA established several field sobriety tests to determine illegal drug use. (*See* previous discussion on page 8).

# Preliminary Breath Test (PBT)

The preliminary breath test (PBT) is usually offered at the scene of a vehicle stop to estimate BAC levels of motorists. The PBT is part of the implied consent law, and in a few states refusing to take the test can result in a lengthier driver's license suspension. The test is scientifically unreliable because the results are distorted by external factors that are unrelated to alcohol consumption. For example, the PBT is supposed to measure ethanol, but the device often mistakes other chemical components as ethanol, which causes a false reading. The PBT is usually 60-80% accurate. Since the PBT lacks scientific accuracy, the result is not admissible in a criminal proceeding; however, the test is usually admissible in a driver's license suspension hearing.

# Chapter Seven

# Chemical Tests

---

# Objective Fallibility

According to prosecutors, chemical testing is conclusive scientific evidence of alcohol impairment. In reality, each test (blood, breath and urine) has numerous flaws that produce distorted results. Although most states provide the right to an independent chemical test by a qualified person of their choice, defendants are often required to submit to a state-sponsored test prior to receiving an independent test. This chapter highlights the factors that distort test results, as well as the advantages and disadvantages of consenting to or refusing a chemical test.

Every state has an implied consent statute that obligates motorists to provide a chemical specimen if the officer has probable cause to believe the motorist is operating a motor vehicle while under the influence of alcohol or drugs. By operating a vehicle, each motorist implicitly consents to this legal requirement. If a motorist refuses the test, the law imposes more stringent driver's license sanctions. In effect, motorists are forced to choose between statutory requirements and their constitutional rights.

# Implied Consent Law Limitations

Although the implied consent statute presumes that every motorist will provide a chemical specimen to measure their BAC level, police officers are obligated to notify motorists of their legal rights and the ramifications of taking or refusing a chemical test. A faulty advisory is sufficient justification to suppress evidence related to the chemical test. Another possible exception involves confusion over conflicting legal theories, e.g., Miranda rights versus the implied consent statute. The advisement informs defendants of their constitutional rights, whereas the implied consent statute is a waiver of these rights.

Similarly, an honest mistake about the law can be persuasive to exclude negative evidence. The implied consent statute was not intended to punish citizens for their sincere confusion about the law. Finally, there may be instances where the defendant initially refuses a chemical test, and then consents. If the officer refuses to allow a test, the refusal could be excluded from evidence. Although some states allow the defendant to contact an attorney before consenting to a chemical test, there is no constitutional right to consult with counsel.

# Chemical Test Refusal

Although there are circumstances when a motorist is not legally obligated to submit to a chemical test, in most instances, if a police officer asks for a chemical specimen, the motorist must comply or suffer the consequences of a test refusal. Motorists are required to perform the specific chemical test chosen by the officer, and only upon successful completion of a valid result, will an independent chemical test be available. Nevertheless, there are a few instances where the defendant is legally entitled to refuse a chemical test.

First, a motorist has the right to request documentation of the blood technician's credentials. Health and safety concerns often outweigh the state's right to gather evidence. Second, a motorist has the right to protest the signing of a hospital liability waiver form. The fact that the motorist is requesting a blood test does not constitute a waiver of all legal claims against the hospital or its personnel. Third, physical limitations justify a chemical test refusal, such as having asthma when asked to take a breath test. However, at the time a chemical test is offered, the motorist must notify the officer of any limitations to allow adequate time for an alternate test.

# Breath Test - Equipment Errors

The chemical breath test is most common among law enforcement officers to determine blood-alcohol concentration. It is easy to use, inexpensive, and an efficient way of processing alleged drunk drivers. On the other hand, breath tests are the least reliable form of testing because numerous chemicals and compounds will distort the test result.

**Chemical Compound Errors.** The infrared breath tests measure ethyl alcohol, but methyl is also confused as ethanol. There are approximately 100 compounds within the human breath at any given time, and 70-80% of these compounds have methyl as a molecular structure. Inevitably, the chemical breath test will produce an unjustifiably higher BAC level. Moreover, breath test results are influenced by the exposure to chemicals, such as paints and solvents, glues and adhesives, or varnish and lacquer.

**False Assumptions.** The chemical breath test falsely assumes that the defendant's BAC is at the peak level of absorption when the sample is drawn. However, since it usually takes one to

# Chart 5

## Alcohol Distribution at Equilibrium

| Tissue or Fluid | Distribution Ratio |
| --- | --- |
| Whole Blood | 1.00 |
| Blood Plasma | 1.15 |
| Brain | 0.85 |
| Liver | 0.90 |
| Skeletal Muscle | 0.85 |
| Saliva | 1.10 |
| Urine | 1.35 |
| Alveolar Breath | 0.00048 (i.e., 1:2100) |

**Note:** Illustrates the average alcohol distribution ratios of various body tissues and fluids at equilibrium.

---

three hours to distribute alcohol throughout the body, there is a significant discrepancy in BAC levels at various body locations. (*See* Chart 5). Although venous blood is a more accurate indicator of brain impairment, during peak absorption the BAC level of arterial blood is higher so the chemical breath test will have a disproportionately higher BAC result.

**Undigested Alcohol.**  Surprisingly enough, undigested alcohol in the mouth can dramatically distort BAC levels because the chemical breath test result will measure alcohol in the lungs *and* mouth.  Finally, there are numerous products on the market that contain alcohol, such as breath fresheners and mouthwash. Although the effects diminish 10-20 minutes after consumption, ingestion immediately prior to a breath test can distort the result. Since most cough syrups also contain alcohol, ingestion at the time of a vehicle stop will cause alcohol to be absorbed into the bloodstream, which will distort the chemical breath test result.  (*See* Chart 6).

---

*DRUNK DRIVING*

## Chart 6
## Alcohol Content of Cough and Breath Products

| Product | % of Alcohol |
|---|---|
| *Cough/cold remedies* | |
| Contact Nightime | 25 |
| Nyquil | 25 |
| Comtrex liquid | 20 |
| Vicks Formula 44M | 20 |
| Vicks Formula 44 | 10 |
| Tylenol Multi-Symptom | 7.0 |
| Triaminic Expectorant | 5.0 |
| Robitussin | 3.5 |
| Dimetapp D.M. | 2.3 |
| *Mouthwash* | |
| Astring-O-Sol | 76 |
| Listerine | 27 |
| Scope (original mint) | 19 |
| Close-Up | 14.5 |
| Signal | 14.5 |
| Cepacol (regular) | 14 |
| Plax | 7.5 |
| Listermint | 6.5 |
| *Throat spray* | |
| N'ICE (mint) | 26 |
| Chloraseptic (original mint) | 19 |
| Sucrets (cherry) | 12 |

# Breath Test - Scientific Errors

The purpose of chemical breath tests is to establish a BAC level in the body. In most states, if a chemical test is administered within a reasonable time after the vehicle stop, the result is presumed to be the BAC level at the time of driving. However, the defendant is allowed to rebut this evidence by proving that the chemical test result is distorted. The following discussion illustrates several challenges to the accuracy of a chemical breath test result.

**Absorption Rates.**  Always consider the time at which a breath test is administered because the BAC result could be inflated.  Since alcohol absorbs into the bloodstream for approximately 50 minutes after the cessation of drinking, breath test results often indicate peak levels, instead of the actual BAC level at the time of driving.  Alcohol absorption rates also increase with cold temperatures, stress, emotional disturbances, exercise, pain or trauma.  Thus, by the time a breath test is administered, the BAC level will be significantly higher than the actual BAC level at the time of driving.

**Metabolic Rates.**  The rate at which the body metabolizes alcohol is critical to establishing BAC levels.  Since individuals have different physiological compositions, the body can metabolize alcohol either slowly or rapidly.  Unfortunately, drunk driving laws assume a fixed rate of alcohol dissipation, when in fact the BAC level can vary significantly depending upon the person's metabolic rate.  As a precaution, use discretion when estimating BAC levels based upon body weight and alcohol consumption.  (*See* Charts 2 and 3).

**Blood.**  Similar to undigested alcohol, the presence of blood in the mouth can distort chemical breath test results.  A cut lip, or mouth incisions/sores elevate BAC levels because the breath test will measure alcohol in the lungs *and* mouth.

**Belching/Hiccups.**  Belching or hiccups can distort chemical breath test results.  The test must be administered at least 10-15 minutes *after* belching, hiccups, regurgitation or vomiting.  If the officer fails to have the defendant under constant observation, then the presence of only one bodily function may be sufficient to suppress the chemical breath test result.

**Margin of Error.** Chemical testing equipment has a 5% margin of error. The standard margin of error has been incorporated into some state laws to avoid judicial dismissals based upon scientific inaccuracies. If a chemical test result is within the margin of error for a specific testing device, it is often inadmissible in a driver's license suspension hearing or criminal trial.

**Other Factors.** Chemical breath tests should not be given to persons wearing dentures because alcohol can remain lodged in the cracks and emanating vapors could distort test results. Body temperature can also influence chemical test results. Generally, for every two degree increase in body temperature the chemical breath test registers a seven percent higher BAC level. The distortion is greater when the mouth has a high humidity level that often accompanies a fever.

Another concern is ensuring that a clean mouthpiece is used in the equipment. Alcohol vapors that remain trapped in the mouthpiece will increase BAC test results. In addition, radio wave interference can distort chemical breath test results.

Acetaldehyde, often present in oral contraceptives, distorts breath test results, and pregnant women have higher levels of the chemical in their bodies. Furthermore, since the human body internally manufactures alcohol, which can skew test results, a conviction could wrongfully occur even though the person did not consume enough alcohol to be considered legally intoxicated.

# Right to Independent Chemical Test

An independent chemical test allows the motorist to select a qualified medical professional, who is not affiliated with the government, to administer a BAC analysis. Most states give motorists the right to demand an independent blood test but only *after* submitting to a chemical test of the officer's choice. The motorist must successfully complete the officer's chosen chemical test to earn the right to an alternate test. If the officer fails to comply with this statutory right, the original chemical test result is usually inadmissible in court.

# Consequences of Sobriety Testing

When the prosecution lacks a chemical test result and only has minimal subjective evidence, it is very difficult to convict the motorist of drunk driving. The denial of all testing--field sobriety, PBT and chemical--will offer the best advantage at a criminal trial. Since the likelihood of a criminal conviction is diminished, the defendant can avoid most of the severe punishment--hefty fines, jail, probation, and most importantly, a criminal record that could haunt a motorist for 15 years. Even the most cautious person could foresee another arrest within that period of time. Naturally, there are legal consequences associated with asserting your legal and constitutional rights.

**Test Refusal.** Although there are benefits to refusing all testing, the motorist usually suffers a lengthier driver's license suspension. The defendant can challenge the legitimacy of the suspension because the arresting officer lacks hard evidence of intoxication, but in most instances the department of transportation will uphold the sanction. Finally, if convicted, the motorist could suffer a slightly longer jail sentence or heftier fine.

**Performing Field Sobriety Tests.** As the number of failed sobriety tests increase, the ability to win an acquittal will decrease. Although the FSTs are subject to effective rebuttal and the PBT result is inadmissible, failed tests provide the prosecution with more incriminating evidence. Nevertheless, it is the chemical test result that is the most devastating evidence.

**Chemical Test Result.** In most drunk driving cases, the chemical test result thwarts most chances of an acquittal. If the BAC level is too high, few medical experts can justify the margin of error, and even fewer jurors will acquit. Moreover, drunk driving charges can be filed even though the BAC result is *below* the legal limit. Most statutes allow drunk driving prosecutions if the driver is impaired to *any* extent. Thus, providing a chemical test is no guarantee against a drunk driving charge or criminal conviction.

Lastly, a significant drawback to chemical testing is the added expense. Challenging scientific results is extremely costly in attorney fees and expert testimony. To present the best defense and maximize the chance of acquittal, medical and scientific expert testimony is imperative. In contrast, litigation costs are substantially less when the defendant declines all forms of chemical testing.

# Weighing The Options

Before venturing onto the roadways on an evening that may involve drinking and driving, consider all the possible scenarios, consequences, and options, to avoid a split-second decision at the time of a police stop. Your conduct should be guided by logic and reason because a rash decision will have long-term consequences. Know how to estimate BAC levels (memorize Charts 2 and 3), perform a self-assessment of your condition, fully understand your priorities, consider financial limitations, and determine whether witnesses are available and willing to offer positive testimony.

**Self-Assessment.** There are numerous factors to weigh at the time of a police stop, but the most important consideration is a self-assessment of your condition. Try to reconstruct the evening to assess food consumption, medications or drugs ingested, and other factors that influence alcohol absorption, then reasonably estimate your BAC level. If the estimated BAC is below the legal limit, then performing field sobriety tests and consenting to a PBT and chemical test may be warranted. However, if the estimated BAC exceeds the legal limit, then it may be advisable to refuse all police testing. Performing any sobriety tests could have detrimental consequences.

**Know Your Priorities.** If there is serious concern about spending a night in jail, then some level of cooperation may be appropriate. However, be aware that providing too much information will result in an arrest and practically guarantees a conviction. When deciding to protect your constitutional rights, consider all the options, including financial ability to support a complete legal defense. When in doubt, many motorists find it best to remain silent and let their lawyer do the talking.

**Legal Defense Costs.** One unfortunate reality about the justice system is the financial burden of protecting and enforcing constitutional rights. For most defendants, the expense must be weighed against future costs associated with a conviction--higher insurance rates, hefty fines, court costs, ignition interlock device, vehicle impoundment, license reinstatement fees, jail sentence, probation, substance abuse treatment, and enhanced criminal penalties and civil sanctions for future offenses. Another cruel reality is that money buys justice. Naturally, the defendant has a greater opportunity for acquittal when larger sums of money are spent on criminal defense. Thus, every motorist should assess all available financial resources to determine the amount they are willing to commit toward defending a drunk driving charge.

**Witnesses.** When deciding whether to submit to a chemical test, consider the number of witnesses available to testify on your behalf. If there are passengers in the vehicle, it may be advantageous to perform field sobriety tests because witness testimony can rebut the officer's observations. The best defense incorporates eyewitness testimony because passengers provide persuasive testimony of the driver's sobriety. Other potential witnesses include a cell mate, bondsman, and anyone observing the defendant prior to or immediately after the arrest. If the defendant was given a telephone call, the recipient should be questioned, especially when it involves a conversation with an attorney. The attorney's testimony would be highly persuasive at trial because it represents an unbiased report to discredit the officer's allegation that the defendant exhibited verbal indicators of intoxication.

**PBT Result.** Motorists have the right to refuse a PBT. When deciding whether to take the chemical test, some motorists use the PBT result to guide their actions. If the result is close to the legal limit, then a chemical test remains a viable option; however, a high BAC is a warning not to provide a chemical test at the station. Unfortunately, this course of action has potentially serious ramifications, such as a driver's license suspension and a potentially harsher criminal penalty. Moreover, the officer is not obligated to reveal the PBT result, so the motorist must assume that the officer will not over-inflate the BAC result.

**Involuntary Blood Test.** An involuntary blood test is administered when a motorist is unconscious or unable to voluntarily consent to a chemical test. Generally, police officers have the legal authority to compel motorists into providing a blood sample for chemical testing purposes.

# Controlling BAC Levels

Since it is perfectly legal to drink and drive--it is only unlawful when driving abilities are impaired--it is important to understand how motorists can control their BAC level to make the roads safe for everyone.

**Consume Food.** Although experts disagree whether it is best to consume protein and carbohydrates, or fats and carbohydrates, the best advice is a well-balanced meal. Instead of eating specific foods, just remember that a full stomach will reduce the rate of alcohol absorption into the bloodstream. Also remember that a closer time span between eating and drinking will have a greater impact on reducing alcohol absorption. As the period of time extends, the effect on alcohol absorption decreases, and after four hours the food has no effect.

**Other Substances.** Studies indicate that nicotine slows alcohol absorption, so smokers have a distinct advantage over nonsmokers, at least in this respect. In addition, higher zinc levels in the body will cause slower alcohol metabolism rates; conversely, alcohol metabolizes faster in people with zinc deficiencies.

# Chapter Eight

# Criminal Defenses

# Legal Rights

This chapter offers legal exceptions to the drunk driving laws and acceptable defenses that may be asserted to avoid a conviction. By asserting these claims, the motorist does not necessarily deny being intoxicated, but asserts a valid reason for breaking the law to rationalize driving in an impaired condition.

There are five common legal excuses--necessity, entrapment, duress, mistake of fact, and lawfully prescribed medication--but other excuses, though often inapplicable to drunk driving charges, may be available to a defendant. Thus, it is necessary to understand the legal rights of motorists because individual circumstances may warrant using one of these defenses in the future.

## Necessity

The defense of necessity requires some urgent event that prompts a motorist to choose between the lesser of two evils, one of which is driving drunk. To qualify for this defense the driver must be avoiding imminent danger to life or property, the danger must be immediate, and the driving must occur before the danger has passed. Moreover, the driver must admit to driving drunk at the time of the incident.

# Entrapment

There is relatively little case law discussing entrapment as a defense to drunk driving because it is unlikely that police officers could lure a person into drinking and then entice the drunkard into driving. Entrapment requires the police to create an environment that lures bystanders into criminal activity. In the drunk driving context, it is highly unlikely that police conduct would ever constitute entrapment.

# Duress

Like the defense of entrapment, duress is equally rare and highly unlikely to arise in the drunk driving context. The factual circumstances would require police officers to knowingly coerce an individual, through violence or comparable threats, to drive a vehicle in a drunken condition. For the person to leave the scene, the officer's threat must be more than a mere order or directive--it must be substantial and the physical violence significant.

# Mistake of Fact

Mistake of fact is a legal defense requiring an honest and reasonable belief that the defendant was not intoxicated. If the reasonable belief was true and accurate, the resulting conduct is considered lawful and proper. In fact, a motorist could allege a mistaken belief about the impact of a certain drug on their ability to drive. For instance, if there is evidence the motorist consumed driving ability, and there was no reason to anticipate or otherwise know the effects, the defendant can use this defense to challenge a drunk driving charge.

# Medication

Operating a motor vehicle while under the influence of a drug is sufficient to establish a drunk driving charge, even if the drug is lawful, over-the-counter, or physically necessary. The only legal requirement is that the drug impairs driving abilities. However, there is one exception where it may be lawful to operate a motor vehicle: 1) if the drug was lawfully prescribed by a licensed medical practitioner; 2) the appropriate dosage was consumed without alcohol; and 3) the patient was not notified that driving was prohibited.

# Chapter Nine

# Substance Abuse

---

# Evaluation and Treatment

In most drunk driving cases, the defendant is ordered to obtain a substance abuse evaluation and complete all recommended treatment. This can range from a drunk driving course to in-patient care, which could cost anywhere between $100 and $10,000. Most judges will order an evaluation within days of the arrest, or immediately schedule an appointment at a state-sponsored facility. In either instance, consult an attorney beforehand because the evaluation will significantly impact the case and personal finances. In some instances, the court does not enforce the deadline or the defendant is allowed to obtain an evaluation from a counselor of their choice.

Since the purpose of an evaluation is to determine whether the defendant has a drinking problem, it is imperative to present the best self-image to minimize the consequences of a negative evaluation. Since judges and prosecutors rely upon the report when determining punishment, it is even more essential to find a sympathetic counselor who offers fair and reasonable evaluations. Any attorney specializing in drunk driving defense will have a list of recommended counselors.

**First Offense.** Upon conviction for first offense drunk driving, many jurisdictions require the defendant to attend a drunk driving course. Proof of completion is often required by the department of transportation before driving privileges are reinstated. If the BAC test result is more than twice the legal limit, the court usually orders a substance abuse evaluation and mandates completion of all recommended treatment.

**Second Offense.** Upon conviction for second offense drunk driving, the court usually requires a substance abuse evaluation and the completion of all recommended treatment. If the recommendation includes commitment to a substance abuse treatment facility, the defendant usually receives credit for time served. Although the court can specify the length of stay, it frequently relies upon the recommendation of the evaluating facility to determine when the defendant has received the maximum benefit from treatment.

**Third or Subsequent Offense.** Although some states specify punishment for drunk driving charges beyond the third offense, most jurisdictions offer the same punishment for all subsequent incidents. Upon conviction for a third or subsequent drunk driving offense, the substance abuse requirements are typically the same as a second offense criminal charge. The defendant must undergo an evaluation and complete all recommended treatment.

# Initial Evaluation

As part of the initial appearance, the judge typically orders an evaluation to determine whether the defendant has a substance abuse problem. Unfortunately, this seemingly innocuous report will heavily influence the prosecutor's recommendation and the judge's sentence. Since the evaluation plays such a critical role in the punishment portion of a drunk driving charge, defendants should approach it with the same degree of seriousness.

**Advance Preparation.** Before speaking with a counselor, every defendant should contemplate answers to common substance abuse questions. Most counselors follow a standard questionnaire to evaluate substance abuse problems. Each answer is scored, and the cumulative sum is compared to a chart that lists various treatment options. Since a lower score translates into less recommended therapy, an ill-prepared defendant may be characterized as a chronic substance abuser who needs prolonged treatment.

**Standard Questions.** Counselors search for answers that indicate a substance abuse problem. Here is a list of typical standardized questions used by counselors. Carefully contemplate an appropriate response prior to undergoing a substance abuse evaluation.

1. Do you binge drink (often 4 drinks or more in one sitting)?
2. Do you drink alone?
3. Do you only drink on special occasions (holidays, weddings, birthdays)?
4. Have you ever experienced blackouts (lost memory from the night before)?
5. Does your family have a history of alcoholism or substance abuse?
6. At what age did you begin consuming alcohol?
7. How often do you consume alcohol per week or per month?
8. Have you ever used illegal substances, and the frequency of use?
9. Do you have any prior legal or substance abuse-related offenses?
10. Have you had prior substance abuse treatment?

Obviously, common sense can properly answer these questions to avoid the appearance of having a substance abuse problem. Here is one client's response:

1. Never binge drinks.
2. Never drinks alone.
3. Does not usually drink on special occasions.
4. Never experienced blackouts.
5. No family history of alcoholism.
6. 21.
7. 2-3 times per month.
8. No illegal substances used.
9. No prior legal or substance abuse-related offenses.
10. No prior substance abuse treatment.

These answers indicate the defendant does not have a substance abuse problem.

**Confidential Evaluation.** Some defendants are concerned that dishonest responses can be verified through public records. Although substance abuse evaluations are confidential, that does not prevent the evaluating institution from using its past records to find inconsistencies or reveal past substance abuse treatment. An untruthful defendant could be caught in a lie, which may lead to contempt of court or additional criminal charges. Although it may be impossible to prove deception on questions 1-8, records may exist on questions 5-6, and 8-10. Counselors will not search public records for contradictory evidence, but if the defendant had three prior drunk driving convictions, and the counselor only recommends minimum treatment, then the prosecutor and judge will realize the defendant lied on the evaluation.

**Release of Information.** The substance abuse evaluation is confidential, so defendants should only authorize release of its contents to their attorney. Since substance abuse evaluations are subjective, a negative recommendation could result in a harsher criminal sentence. By only authorizing the release of information to the defense attorney, there remains an option of selecting a different counselor to obtain a more favorable evaluation. If the evaluation is reasonable, then the defendant can authorize the counselor to release information to other court officials. By shopping for the best evaluation, the defendant is likely to receive a more lenient sentence.

# Appendix A

# GLOSSARY

**actual possession:** Immediate occupancy or direct physical control over an object.

**administrative law judge:** Person presiding over an administrative hearing with the power to administer oaths, take testimony, rule on evidentiary matters, and make determinations of factual issues.

**black-and-white fever:** Nervous condition that frequently occurs in motorists who have been followed by a police officer for a lengthy period of time, causing them to drive erratically because of intense concentration on the rearview mirror instead of the road.

**constructive possession:** Possession that is assumed to exist, where the person has sufficient, though not actual, physical control over the object.

**controlled substance:** Any drug specifically designated by the government as narcotic, or other chemicals that are illegal without a prescription.

**conviction:** Public record certifying personal responsibility for a crime. A conviction occurs with a guilty verdict, plea of guilty, or no contest plea. Regardless of the legal distinctions, in the eyes of the law, each is treated as a conviction. The only exception is the granting of a deferred judgment or other official act that expunges the criminal record or renders the final judgment void.

**deferred judgment:** When a conviction is removed from the defendant's criminal record after successfully completing a probationary term. There is usually no imprisonment or fine.

**deferred sentence:** Criminal sentence is postponed, usually until the defendant fulfills certain obligations imposed by the court. It is not the same as a suspended sentence.

**divided-attention tests:** Field sobriety tests that require the defendant to perform tasks requiring simultaneous mental and physical activities, such as the one-leg lift or walk-the-line test.

**driver's license suspension:** Length of time a motorist is denied the privilege of lawfully driving. *See* Note at end of glossary.

**field sobriety tests:** Procedure used by law enforcement personnel to determine the alcohol impairment of drivers. There are three standardized tests, which range from physical coordination and verbal articulation to divided-attention activities and involuntary responses.

**hard suspension:** Length of time a driver's license is suspended where a motorist is not entitled to drive or receive a temporary restricted license.

**horizontal gaze nystagmus (HGN):** Standardized field sobriety test that monitors the involuntary jerking of the eyes. An object is placed six inches from the eyes and slowly moved in various directions until reaching a 45-degree angle.

**implied consent:** Statutory requirement in the drunk driving laws that obligates motorists, who operate a motor vehicle within the state, to provide a chemical specimen that measures BAC levels. The law imposes a driver's license sanction for a chemical test failure or refusal.

**initial appearance:** Usually the first court appearance where the defendant is advised of the alleged criminal charges and constitutional rights. Bail/bond is set, conditions of release are established, and a preliminary hearing date is scheduled.

**joint civil liability:** Where all the parties are subject to civil liability for the same debt; if one or more person cannot afford the debt, the other(s) must pay that share.

**license suspension:** *see* driver's license suspension.

**Miranda advisement (Miranda rights):** The fifth amendment constitutional right against self-incrimination, having an attorney present, or receiving a court-appointed attorney. Police officers must advise defendants of these rights at the time of arrest. If a defendant is taken into custody or experiences a significant deprivation of freedoms, and no waiver of rights is provided, all subsequent admissions are inadmissible at trial.

**preliminary hearing:** Court proceeding where a judge determines whether there is probable cause that the defendant committed the crime as charged.

**reality-based substance abuse education program:** Supervised tours of hospitals, treatment facilities or morgues to illustrate the consequences of drunk driving.

**suspended sentence:** Formal sentence where the judge reduces or eliminates some period of incarceration, provided the defendant successfully completes a probationary period.

**suspension:** *see* driver's license suspension.

**temporary restricted license (TRL):** Driving permit that authorizes a motorist to operate motor vehicles despite their driving privileges being suspended, but it only allows traveling to specified places, such as maintaining employment or continuing health care. A TRL cannot be used for pleasure driving.

**white-line fever:** Condition that frequently occurs after driving a lengthy period of time where the driver becomes hypnotized by the road and often weaves within the lane of traffic.

**work permit:** *see* temporary restricted license.

**zero tolerance:** Underage motorist with a BAC often ranging between .02% and .10%. Adopted by state legislatures in an effort to curb underage drinking and driving.

**Note:** For purposes of this book, most references to a driver's license suspension will encompass every status of a person's driving privileges, whether suspended, revoked, denied or barred.

# Appendix B

# ABBREVIATIONS

**ALJ:**    administrative law judge

**BAC:**    blood-alcohol concentration

**DOT:**    department of transportation

**FST:**    field sobriety test

**HGN:**    horizontal gaze nystagmus

**IID:**    ignition interlock device

**NHTSA:**    National Highway Traffic Safety Administration

**PBT:**    preliminary breath test

**TRL:**    temporary restricted license (often referred to as a work permit)

# INDEX